EXTREME SPORTS EVENTS

ULTRA-TRAIL MARATHON DU MONT-BLANC

KELLY FENG

SportsZone
An Imprint of Abdo Publishing
abdobooks.com

abdobooks.com

Published by Abdo Publishing, a division of ABDO, PO Box 398166, Minneapolis, Minnesota 55439. Copyright © 2024 by Abdo Consulting Group, Inc. International copyrights reserved in all countries. No part of this book may be reproduced in any form without written permission from the publisher. SportsZone™ is a trademark and logo of Abdo Publishing.

Printed in the United States of America, North Mankato, Minnesota.
102023
012024

Cover Photo: Yannis Kontos/Polaris/Newscom
Interior Photos: Jeff Pachoud/AFP/Getty Images, 4–5, 7, 10–11, 25, 29; Laurent Cipriani/AP Images, 6, 13, 14, 23, 28; Patrick McDermott/Getty Images for Canyons UTMB/Getty Images Sport/Getty Images, 9; Jean-Pierre Clatot/AFP/Getty Images, 16–17; Red Line Editorial, 18; Ania Freindorf/Sipa/AP Images, 21; Olly Bowman/DPPI/LiveMedia/NurPhoto/AP Images, 27

Editor: Steph Giedd
Series Designer: Cynthia Della-Rovere

Library of Congress Control Number: 2023939472

Publisher's Cataloging-in-Publication Data

Names: Feng, Kelly, author.
Title: Ultra-Trail du Mont-Blanc / by Kelly Feng
Description: Minneapolis, Minnesota: Abdo Publishing, 2024 | Series: Extreme sports events | Includes online resources and index.
Identifiers: ISBN 9781098292393 (lib. bdg.) | ISBN 9798384910336 (ebook)
Subjects: LCSH: Extreme sports--Juvenile literature. | Action sports (Extreme sports)--Juvenile literature. | Ultra-marathon running--Juvenile literature. | Foot races--Juvenile literature. | Mountain ranges--Juvenile literature. | Blanc, Mont (France and Italy)--Juvenile literature.
Classification: DDC 796.046--dc23

TABLE OF CONTENTS

CHAPTER 1
Steep Hills and Stunning Views 4

CHAPTER 2
Lay of the Land 10

CHAPTER 3
Scale the Trail...................... 16

CHAPTER 4
Testing Limits...................... 22

Glossary 30
More Information..............31
Online Resources 31
Index...............................32
About the Author 32

CHAPTER 1

STEEP HILLS AND STUNNING VIEWS

It's race day in Chamonix, France, a popular mountain resort town. Chamonix is a village at the base of a mountain called Mont Blanc. At 15,771 feet (4,807 m), Mont Blanc is the highest mountain in western Europe. There is excitement in the air. The town square is decorated with flowers and flags representing countries around the world. Hundreds of onlookers line the streets waiting for the Ultra-Trail du Mont-Blanc (UTMB) festivities to begin at 6:00 p.m. Nearby, more than 2,000 runners stand behind the starting line, many wearing sunglasses and visors.

Runners take off from the UTMB starting line in Chamonix, France, in 2022.

The start of the UTMB can be crowded as more than 2,000 runners eagerly await the beginning of the race.

The air is sticky and humid but will turn cool at dusk. Regardless, the runners are eager to begin.

Among the runners is Audrée Lafrenière, a 36-year-old trail runner from Vancouver, British Columbia. Lafrenière is no beginner. She has been running long distances for many years. With her training, she is ready for the 106-mile (171-km) ultramarathon.

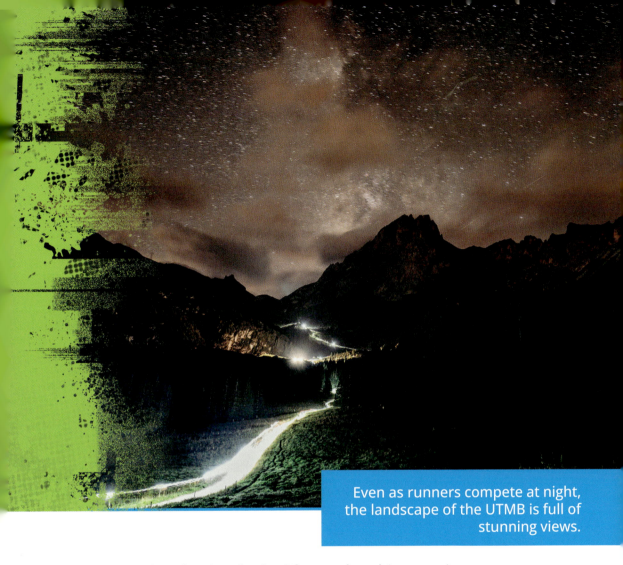

Even as runners compete at night, the landscape of the UTMB is full of stunning views.

Lafrenière has looked forward to this race since visiting Chamonix in 2018. Winning the UTMB is not Lafrenière's goal. She feels she has already won, because she was selected to compete in the biggest race of her life. Tears stream down her face as she waits. Lafrenière is overwhelmed by a mixture of nervousness and happiness. She looks at the runners gathered around her. Each one of them has worked hard to get to the UTMB.

The crowd starts a rhythmic clapping, shouting encouragement. A digital display counts down the seconds until the race begins. And then the moment has arrived. Lafrenière's tears disappear, and she looks straight ahead. Before she knows it, she follows a swarm of runners taking their first strides in the UTMB.

ELEVATE THE EXPERIENCE

The UTMB is an ultramarathon, which is any footrace longer than a standard marathon of 26.2 miles (42.2 km). The UTMB course allows participants to run through the mountains in a unique environment. The 106-mile course makes a loop through France, Italy, and Switzerland. The race ends back where it began, in Chamonix.

Though the mountain is beautiful, it can be dangerous. Running the UTMB can be treacherous as runners navigate rough and uneven surfaces, slippery slopes, steep hills, and loose stones. In addition to navigating tricky terrain, UTMB runners reach a maximum height of more than 8,200 feet (2,500 m) above sea level. The runners must be prepared to cope with the mountain weather, which can vary greatly. They might encounter blazing heat or bone-chilling rain.

Runners may finish in less than 20 hours or closer to 46 hours and 30 minutes, the race cutoff time. Regardless of their speed, runners share the same experience on

The UTMB World Series Canyons Endurance Run in California is one of many qualifying races for the UTMB World Series Finals in Chamonix.

the same exceptional course. The event began in 2003 and has grown more popular each year since. Now the UTMB is considered the world's leading trail event. And the race's popularity even led to the creation of the UTMB World Series circuit, a series of trail races held in locations around the world, including Thailand, China, New Zealand, Australia, Spain, and Austria.

CHAPTER 2

LAY OF THE LAND

The UTMB is one of the largest trail-running events, capped at around 2,300 racers. Runners worldwide apply for a chance to compete in the race. As the UTMB grew in popularity, officials accepted more runners and tightened standards. But the number of qualified applicants continued to increase. After the registration system filled within eight minutes in 2008, a lottery system was created.

To qualify for this race, runners must have achieved specific race requirements, beginning with earning at least one "Running Stone." Running Stones are collected by participating in other UTMB World Series races. Different numbers of Running Stones are awarded to finishers of the various UTMB World Series

Some racers use trekking poles to prevent injuries to their joints.

11

races, depending on the course's difficulty. The UTMB World Series offers races of different difficulties—12.4 miles (20 km), 31.1 miles (50 km), 62.1 miles (100 km), and 100 miles (161 km). These measurements factor in both the length and the total elevation gain of each course. One Running Stone is good for one entry into the UTMB lottery to run in the UTMB World Series Finals, which includes the original UTMB, among other races.

Only runners who have earned at least one Running Stone in the last two years can enter the UTMB lottery. In addition, they must also have a valid UTMB Index to race. The UTMB Index is an equation created to measure the performance level of trail runners around the world. The equation is based on their results from participating in UTMB World Series races. To enter the lottery, runners need to have a UTMB Index in one of the two longest race categories. And they need to have earned that Index in the past two years for it to be considered valid.

TRAINING AND NUTRITION

Before beginning ultramarathon training, an athlete should be able to run for at least an hour. Runners must also allow for at least six months of training before entering a race. While there is no set training plan for the UTMB, runners do certain training exercises to be ready for this race.

Competitors never know what they'll encounter during the race, so they must be ready for anything.

Though this is a running race, walking training is just as important. Sometimes conditions are too strenuous for running, so walking is required. This can happen when going up steep hills and down slopes. When runners walk on slopes, they use different muscles than those they use for running on level ground. They should practice walking on steep slopes before race day. Steep downhill slopes increase the impact on a runner's body compared to running on level ground. As a result, many runners use trekking poles during training and races to help with

The high altitude of the mountains can make it difficult to breathe while running. It is important for runners to train in high altitudes so their bodies are prepared.

climbing up hills and to reduce impact on downhill slopes. These poles help to prevent injuries.

Some experts on ultramarathon training recommend that weekends should consist of more intense training. Another name for this intense training is a weekend shock. Athletes train hard for two- to three-day stretches, followed by several days of full recovery. Runners may plan two to six of these weekends, but the weekend shocks shouldn't be scheduled too close to the race. The last one should be about four weeks ahead of the competition. These intense training sessions don't need to focus only on running either. To become used to the demands of the race, runners should mix in walking and a good amount of downhill running.

It is also important for runners to practice high-altitude training, which means running at elevations high above sea level. The air is "thinner" at higher elevations. There is less oxygen in the air, and the air pressure changes. Walking and running at high altitudes will help runners get used to the effects of these changes on the body.

Additionally, athletes should experiment with different nutrition plans to make sure they have the energy they need to compete. Runners need fuel in their diets. Every meal and snack should be based on natural foods with carbohydrates, protein, fats, vitamins, and minerals. Eating more carbohydrates is a great way to help fuel the body. Examples of healthy carbohydrates for runners are whole grains, bread, pasta, barley, cereal, and crackers. Loading up on carbohydrates the day before can lead to digestive issues during the race. So, runners eat more carbohydrates two to three days before the event. The day before a race, they eat less than usual.

CHAPTER 3

SCALE THE TRAIL

Because the race can last up to 46 hours and 30 minutes, runners need to pack a "drop bag" that they will pick up at a checkpoint in Courmayeur, Italy. The drop bag can contain items such as food, first aid equipment, socks, running shoes, and clothing. Additionally, each runner is required to have certain supplies during the race, including a minimum water supply of 34 fluid ounces (1 L), a headlamp, and a smartphone with the LiveRun app installed.

The UTMB trail sends runners counterclockwise through France, Italy, and Switzerland before returning to Chamonix. Along the way, runners pass through 18 villages and catch glimpses of historic mountain huts and plenty of cows, sheep, and goats.

Vests with pockets are one way runners can carry required supplies with them on the course.

ULTRA-TRAIL DU MONT-BLANC

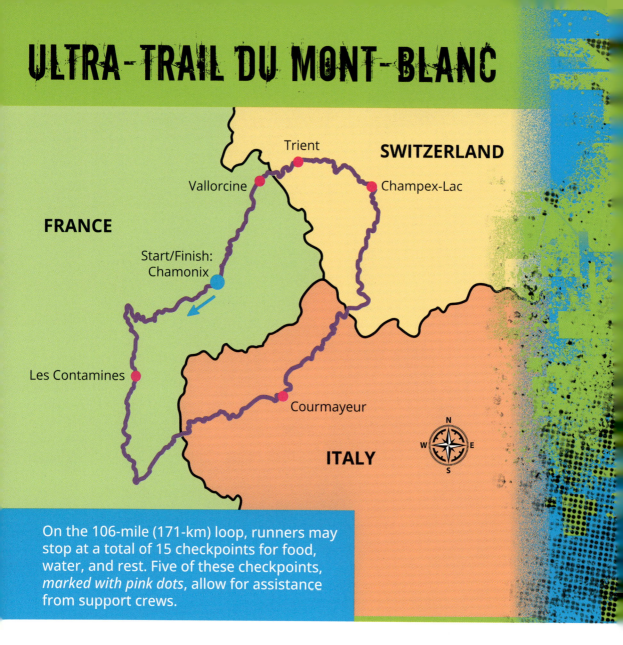

On the 106-mile (171-km) loop, runners may stop at a total of 15 checkpoints for food, water, and rest. Five of these checkpoints, *marked with pink dots*, allow for assistance from support crews.

Runners have an up-close look at France's historic Notre Dame de la Gorge cathedral and Switzerland's Dranse de Ferret river.

Though the route is scenic, Mont Blanc has its challenges. The slopes are so steep that athletes will need to use some energy to slow themselves down while walking or running downhill. The slopes might also be covered with rocks, roots, mud, and water, making them tricky to navigate. In addition, the changing weather and nighttime conditions can make the terrain even more challenging.

Even the most fit runners find themselves dropping out of the race. The surface environment often causes injury. In 2022 British runner Ben Parkes experienced a "nightmare of a race." Early in the race, Parkes hit a tree root while running downhill. The crash caused him to fall onto a jagged rock, injuring the side of his knee. At first, he thought it was a bruise and a scraped knee. But as he continued, he felt a sharp pain, and his knees locked. He was in too much pain to stand, let alone run. The evening had turned to darkness, and Parkes could barely see. But he was wearing a headlamp, which helped him slowly wobble down the hill, find an exit, and seek help.

SIMPLE COMFORTS

In addition to food, drinks, and medical attention, checkpoints have other amenities for racers. For example, at the Courmayeur checkpoint, the Dolonne sports complex has showers and cots to take naps on. However, runners caution against getting too comfortable there. Some runners end up dropping out of the race, lured in by the comforts of a shower and a bed to rest their bodies.

Also in 2022, Canadian Marianne Hogan trailed American Katie Schide for a third of the race. Hogan caught up to Schide at a checkpoint at night and took the lead. However, Hogan injured herself and tore a back muscle. This injury allowed Schide to catch up to Hogan, pass her, and win the race. Still, Hogan became the first Canadian to reach the podium at UTMB, placing second in the women's category.

CHECKPOINTS

Race organizers provide 15 checkpoints throughout the course. For example, the checkpoint at Courmayeur, Italy, helps energize runners by offering healthy foods such as oranges, ham slices, and cheese cubes. It is also one of only two checkpoints to offer any hot foods. And it's the only location where athletes can access their drop bags.

Runners often bring a support crew. This crew helps the runner with the challenging race conditions. Only five of the checkpoints allow crews to provide medical aid to their runners. These designated stations give the runners a chance to receive help with health concerns that have come up along the way. These conditions include dehydration, heat exhaustion, and hypothermia. Dehydration happens when the body doesn't have enough water, causing headaches and dizziness. People may even

Though each UTMB checkpoint offers different services, common examples include food, fluids, and bathrooms. Some even offer a power supply for charging devices.

pass out. To prevent dehydration, runners drink before they get thirsty and carry plenty of fluids and foods high in water, such as fruits and vegetables. Heat exhaustion occurs when the body loses too much water and salt, usually through sweating. Runners wear sunscreen and loose-fitting, lightweight clothing to prevent heat exhaustion. They also make sure to drink plenty of fluids. Hypothermia takes place when the body loses heat faster than it can produce it, causing low body temperature. Runners prevent hypothermia by dressing for the cold. They also keep warm gloves, socks, and clothing in their drop bags.

CHAPTER 4

TESTING LIMITS

To reach the finish line, racers must get through the Chamonix town center, where they hear a backdrop of cowbells ringing and loud cheering. Adoring fans lean over metal barriers, hoping to give the runners a high five. Supporters wave flags or raise their arms. Many record the celebration on their phones.

While many elite runners will focus on their race times, most are happy with simply completing the race. In the 2022 UTMB, there were 2,627 total runners. However, 838 runners withdrew. That means over 30 percent of runners did not finish the race. Some of them dropped out due to strenuous conditions or injury, and others exceeded the cutoff

Xavier Thévenard of France takes in the crowd as he crosses the UTMB finish line in Chamonix in 2018.

time of 46 hours and 30 minutes. Anybody who finishes under the cutoff time sees it as a symbol of pride.

PAIN CAVE

A runner struggling to reach the finish line may need an inner pep talk. A race this long is a mental challenge as much as a physical one. Building up a strong mindset can be just as important for a runner as being physically ready to compete.

Hannah Leith, a 2019 finisher, talked about visiting the "pain cave." The pain cave is a state of mind where runners show how badly they want to finish. When they enter the pain cave, they show their ability to endure. Leith had several strategies to push through her physical limits. She overcame the urges to quit by limiting her time at checkpoints. Leith was also afraid if her legs seized up, she wouldn't finish. To make sure that didn't happen, she decided she would only sit down when she needed to change her shoes or socks.

During the grueling race, Leith dug deep into her mental strength to push through every hour of the race. Although her body wanted to stop, she focused all of her energy on putting one foot in front of the other to keep moving. Leith's quadriceps muscles were so sore that in her last footsteps toward the finish line, she struggled to lift her

It takes an incredible amount of physical and mental strength to finish the UTMB.

legs up. Once she crossed, she was awestruck, relieved, and emotional.

RECOVERY

After the UTMB, athletes take many days or weeks to recover. Physical recovery from the race takes at least two weeks of running easy, short routes after the UTMB. It's important to get in some short runs in addition to resting during recovery to avoid muscles tightening up.

OLDEST FINISHER

The oldest runner to finish the UTMB was 73-year-old Christophe Geiger of Switzerland in 2015. He finished the race just five minutes before the cutoff time. It was his fourth try but his first successful attempt at completing the race.

But recovery will include more rest days than normal. Some runners encourage others to eat a healthy diet and get as much sleep as their bodies need.

American ultrarunner Courtney Dauwalter, who had two straight UTMB wins, also emphasizes recovering mentally. She believes it's essential to recover emotionally when the race is over. Many runners let their bodies rest, but Dauwalter's mental health also needed extra attention. "I'm still running and easy jogging," said Dauwalter. "But I will take time to not stress out for a while before I get ready for the next one."

ONWARD

The UTMB awards the winners with prize money. In 2022 UTMB paid out $10,400 to the male and female winners of the race. Additionally, approximately $5,200 went to second-place finishers and $3,125 for third. Fourth- and fifth-place finishers took home about $1,500, while sixth through tenth earned $1,000. While these amounts are not

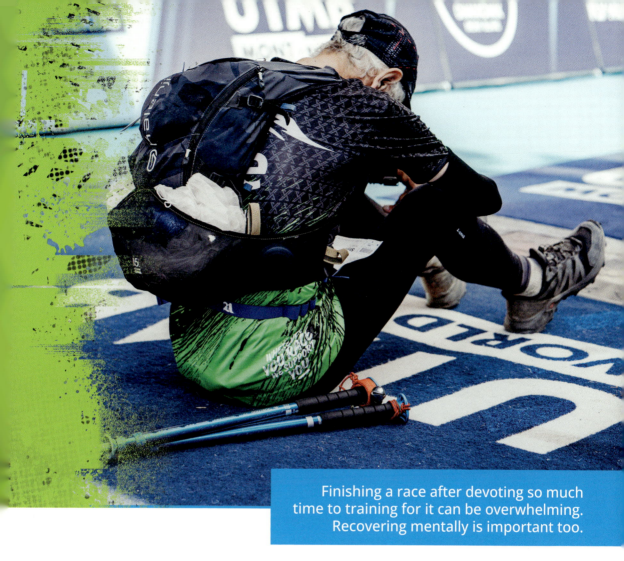

Finishing a race after devoting so much time to training for it can be overwhelming. Recovering mentally is important too.

life-changing, the money often helps athletes pay for fees, training, or traveling.

In addition to prize money, some athletes receive sponsorships. For example, four-time UTMB winner Kilian Jornet from Spain has partnered with several companies to market their products. One example is Strava, a running, cycling, and hiking app. He runs routes using Strava, and other Strava users can keep pace with his

Abdennour Benmammar, *center*, of France was the final competitor to cross the finish line in 2018. Simply completing the UTMB is reward enough for many racers.

Katie Schide of the United States celebrates winning the 2022 UTMB.

training and follow his schedule. However, even though Jornet is well-known in the ultramarathon community, he is in a small group of ultramarathoners who benefit from sponsorships.

Those who enter the UTMB aren't seeking financial gain. They seek the challenge of taking on Mont Blanc, and as ultrarunners, they look for the next thrill. They're motivated by the challenging conditions of the race and the prospect of reaching the finish line. The excitement of the task is enough to spark their desire to sign up for one of the most difficult footraces in the world.

GLOSSARY

altitude
The height of a thing or point above sea level.

carbohydrates
Nutrients found in food that are broken down and converted to use for energy.

cathedral
A church.

elevation
The distance above sea level.

lottery
A prize drawing.

resort
A place that provides entertainment and lodging to visitors.

scenic
Having beautiful natural scenery.

sponsorships
Money given to athletes in return for supporting a company's products publicly.

terrain
The physical qualities of the land within a region.

treacherous
Filled with hazards and dangerous footing.

MORE INFORMATION

BOOKS

Hanlon, Luke. *4 Deserts Ultramarathon Series*. Minneapolis, MN: Abdo Publishing, 2024.

Hewson, Anthony K. *Arrowhead 135*. Minneapolis, MN: Abdo Publishing, 2024.

Hewson, Anthony K. *Badwater 135*. Minneapolis, MN: Abdo Publishing, 2024.

ONLINE RESOURCES

To learn more about the Ultra-Trail du Mont-Blanc, please visit **abdobooklinks.com** or scan this QR code. These links are routinely monitored and updated to provide the most current information available.

INDEX

Chamonix, France, 4, 7–8, 16, 22

Courmayeur, Italy, 16, 19, 20

Dauwalter, Courtney, 26

dehydration, 20–21

Geiger, Christophe, 26

Hogan, Marianne, 20

hypothermia, 20–21

Jornet, Kilian, 27, 29

Lafrenière, Audrée, 6–8

Leith, Hannah, 24

LiveRun, 16

lottery, 10, 12

Mont Blanc, 4, 18, 29

Parkes, Ben, 19

Running Stones, 10, 12

Schide, Katie, 20

Strava, 27

UTMB Index, 12

ABOUT THE AUTHOR

Kelly Feng is a journalist and reporter who has covered gymnastics, speed skating, and football, among other sports. She lives in Milwaukee, Wisconsin, with her family.